Niccolo Paganini

BOY MUSIC GENIUS

Niccolo Paganini

BOY MUSIC GENIUS

ILONA NOGARR

ARPress
ILLUMINATING IDEAS.
EMPOWERING VOICES

ARPress
45 Dan Road Suite 5
Canton MA 02021
Hotline: 1(888) 821-0229
Fax: 1(508) 545-7580

Ordering Information:
Quantity sales. Special discounts are available on quantity purchases by corporations, associations, and others. For details, contact the publisher at the address above.

Printed in the United States of America.

| ISBN-13: | Softcover | 979-8-89356-050-3 |
| | eBook | 979-8-89356-051-0 |

Library of Congress Control Number: 2024903363

I dedicate this book to all musicians, especially to violinists. And to my love for music.

2

The night was rainy and stormy when the little baby boy took his first breath. You could hear the echo of crashing waves in the background. The building he was born in was barely holding together. It was called the Hiding Place for the Poor. All of this neighborhood was filled with people who had a lack of money.

It was late in the year 1782, in Janua, Italy. In translation Janua means The Door. Who could have guessed back then, that this name would become so important, a real door to the world in this baby boys future.

The first years of Niccolos childhood were the best, because he had a chance to spend lots of time with his gentle mother. Most of the time he saw his father in a bad mood. He even heard his father describing him as an ugly creature with a big head and chin, and with unusually long nose and fingers. On the other hand, his mother found his eyes to be amazingly beautiful and bright.

Niccolo was a five-year-old boy, and his big eyes reflected fear toward a grumpy old man. He tried to please him to avoid his anger. That man was his father. And having had little luck in the bank where he worked, his father earned extra income by playing the mandolin. And now it was little Niccolos turn to start being part of making money for the family. Niccolo enjoyed only the moments when a little sparkle came to his fathers eyes, and his usually dissatisfied pursed lips softened with a little smile. That meant Niccolo was doing a good job with his improvements, and this made him try even harder.

After two years of young Niccolo playing mandolin, his father started to see his genius, and moved on to the next instrument the violin. Now his childhood turned from bad to worse. The little dirt-floor basement under the house turned into his own living nightmare,

Niccolo tried to pull his sleeves down more and close the upper button of his shirt, but he knew he was outgrowing it, and there was no way to get his body warmed up. Cold from slightly wet stone walls reached his bones and made him tremble. Spiders were free to make as many nests as they wanted. And darkness almost overpowered the tiny little candlelit room.

The noise of the dropping hatch door brought Niccolo back to his senses. It was not happening for the first time. That was his punishment for missing a note or for not playing the right tune. To get out from the cold room meant making his playing perfect, to practice for hours not knowing when mercy would be coming. Only then could he get out of his misery.

His father could not wait long enough for Niccolos fast improvements, so he took him to various local violinists. Niccolo progresses quickly, past his teachers abilities. Even so, his father became meaner every day. Niccolos body was full of bruises or black-and-blue marks and stripes from his fathers pinching and whipping. His mothers cry for mercy made his fathers response even worse. His father was determined to save money for his old age through his sons performances.

Smelling the money, his father traveled with Niccolo to a bigger city, to seek further directions from Rolla, a famous teacher. After listening to Niccolos outstanding playing, Rolla referred him to his own teacher, Ferdinando.

On the way from city to city Niccolos father made him play, for the money they needed at every stop they made. Very little food and sleepless nights made little Niccolos health weaken. He coughed a lot.

Paganini earned numerous scholarships by age 18, because of his tremendous musical talents. Luckily, he did not feel the pressure from his father anymore. Now he was the one who dove passionately into his own musical world. He had the urge to compose one piece of music after another, which he did extremely well.

Rumors of his genius spread all over the world. Nobody at the time could equal his playing abilities. His created music was so hard to play that he was the only one who could manage it.

Niccolos teacher, Paer, wrote in the newspaper article that Paganini turned a new page in musical history. And now, even today, Paganinis heavenly sounds of highly skilled music have an influence on our modern world of the arts.

Bibliography

1. Anatoly Vinograov – PAGANINI – Publication of Literature, Moscow, 1953.
2. The American Peoples Encyclopedia. A Modern Reference Work
3. Websites: en.wikipedia.org/wiki/Niccolo_Paganini
4. www.answers.com/topic/niccol-paganini
5. www.thirteen.org/publicars/violin.paganini.html
6. www.suite101.com/article.cfmviolin-composers
7. en.wikipedia.org/wiki/14-caprices
8. www.brittanica.com/EBchecked/topic/438172

About the Author

- Ilona Nogarr was born in Põlva, Estonia.
- Started ballet training at age seven.
- Accepted to Tartu Children's Music School major in violin at age ten, also was a member of Elementary School mandolin orchestra and choir.
- Chosen to Põlva Middle School eight girls band as a singer, also to choir, speed skating team, long distance running team, gymnastics team.
- 1966 accepted to Tartu Medical School.

- Took competitive ballroom dance lessons at Tartu City Club in Tartu Estonia.
- 1969 -1970 – studied Fashion Design and Tailoring at Tallinn Fashion House in Tallinn, Estonia.
- 1973 -1977 – studied at Tartu University, major in Rhythmic Gymnastics, which was strongly influenced with Isadora Duncan style. Graduated with honors.
- Was chosen to Tartu University Rhythmic Gymnastics competitive and contemporary dance performing company 1973-1980.
- 1974 -1977 – Was chosen to Tartu University Club Jazz Company and received a solo dancer nomination. Choreographed a dance piece for Tartu University Drama Club.
- Started teaching at Tartu University while a student in 1975, also was teaching pre school dancers.
- 1977 - 1980 – was teaching dance in Tartu Technical High School, also was Assistant Director for after school activities.
- 1980 Performer at Olympic Games opening ceremony (Soviet Union).
- 1986 performed at Goodwill Games opening ceremony in Moscow Russia.
- 1980 - 1984 – was teaching Modern Rhythmic Gymnastics dance at Tallinn Pedagogical Institute in Tallinn, Estonia.
- 1984 - 1989 – was teaching dance at Kirov Sports Club and Tallinn Sport Club.
- From 1989 to January 2022 has been teaching dance in USA- California, Virginia, and Texas. Was the owner and director of European Dance Studio from 1993-2011
- Director and owner of Denison Dance Actually from 2011-January 2022
- Studied at the Institute of Children's Literature from 2009-2011.
- Wrote and illustrated two children's books -- "Niccolo Paganini Boy Music Genius" and "Lola And The Apple".

- Observed ballet classes at American Ballet Theater; New York City Ballet; Washington Ballet; Kirov Ballet Academy in Washington DC; University of North Carolina School of the Arts; Vienna, Austria Ballet School; Oklahoma City Ballet company.
- Attended dance workshops from 1992. Took Jazz workshop with legendary Gus Giordano and Frank Hatchet and David Howard ballet workshop. Attended Dance Teachers Summer Summit in New York.
- 2022 retired from teaching and started ballroom dance at Fred Astaire Studio in North Port, Florida under professional instructors Andre Lecca and Yamila Molina. Also partnered with Andre Lecca at pro/am dance competition and showcase.
- Ilona's students have been receiving high results at dance competitions (Dance Educators of America; American Dance Awards; New York City Dance Alliance ext.)
- Ilona's daughter Darli Iakovleva received a scholarship to Jeoffry Ballet summer intensive twice; was top ten in regional finals at Youth American Grand Prix twice. Competed in New York City at Youth American Grand Prix finals.
- Recently she has retired from professional ballerina at Vanemuine Theatre ballet in Tartu Estonia and opened her own ballet school in Florida.
- Ilona also has two sons- Renal Loit and Ergo Thomson.
- Ilona feels some of her biggest accomplishments was producing a big ballet production as "Nutcracker", "Snow White", "An Awakening" and "Sleeping Beauty". Also, she feels blessed to have had the opportunity to mold her students to disciplined, focused, responsible and self-confident personalities which is helpful in any profession they will choose. They will appreciate the arts for the rest of their life.

- She feels her separation from others is the variety of different arts she has studied and the fact that she can make the performing costumes herself, as well as props. She can choreograph and stage as well as teach all styles of dance.
- Ilona is also involved in City Art Club activities.
- Ilona has also been acting with the City of Sherman Community Players in Sherman, Texas in "Three Musketeers" as Queen Anne. She also choreographed a tap dance for the City of Sherman Community Players "Drowsy Chaperone" in Sherman, Texas, which received a great review from Joel Taylor, Associate Critic for John Garcia's The Column.
- She believes that life is to be lived with passion, with respect and love towards other fellows and to stay close to God